THE
PLANT HUNTERS

THE PLANT HUNTERS

True Stories of Their Daring Adventures to the Far Corners of the Earth

Anita Silvey

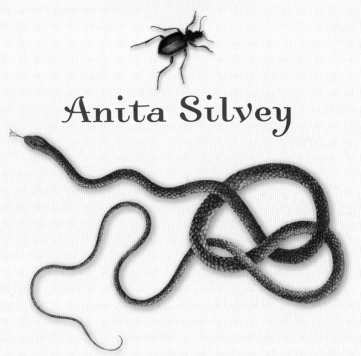

FARRAR STRAUS GIROUX / NEW YORK

Text copyright © 2012 by Anita Silvey
Distributed in Canada by D&M Publishers, Inc.
Printed in China
by Toppan Leefung Printing Ltd.,
Dongguan City, Guangdong Province
Designed by Carol Goldenberg
First edition, 2012
1 3 5 7 9 10 8 6 4 2

mackids.com

Library of Congress Cataloging-in-Publication Data
Silvey, Anita.
    The plant hunters : true stories of their daring adventures to the far corners of the
Earth / Anita Silvey.
        p. cm.
    ISBN: 978-0-374-30908-4
    1. Plant collectors—Biography—Juvenile literature. 2. Plant collecting—History—
Juvenile literature. I. Title.

QK26.S57 2011
580.75—dc22

2011005161

FOR MY SISTER LISA SILVEY

who takes delight in the natural world

CONTENTS

"Botanomania": A Passion for Plants / 3

CHAPTER 1: The Indiana Jones of the Nineteenth Century / 6

CHAPTER 2: Why Did They Do It? / 17

CHAPTER 3: Bringing the Plants Home Alive / 32

CHAPTER 4: Bringing Themselves Home Alive / 43

CHAPTER 5: Plant Superstars / 52

CHAPTER 6: Contemporary Plant Geeks / 65

Time Line / 70

Author's Note / 73

Notes / 75

Bibliography / 79

Illustration Credits / 82

Index / 83

THE
PLANT HUNTERS

Etab. Lith. de L. Stroobant, à Gand

Colored lithograph of an orchid created by Belgian artist Jean Jules Linden in the late 1800s. In the collection of the author.

"BOTANOMANIA": A PASSION FOR PLANTS

ONE GOT EATEN by tigers in the Philippines; one died of fever in Ecuador; one drowned in the Orinoco River; one fell to his death in Sierra Leone. Another survived rheumatism, pleurisy, and dysentery while sailing the Yangtze River in China, only to be murdered later. A few ended their days in lunatic asylums; many simply vanished into thin air.

Those who survived endured all kinds of challenges. Vampire bats sucked on their toes; bears attacked them in the woods. These intrepid adventurers faced slime pits, snowdrifts, river rapids, floods, and avalanches. They fell into fitful sleep at night in jungles, listening to the deafening chattering and screeching of wild animals. The sun burned them by day; the cold seeped into their bones at night. They were racked by fever.

Who were these adventurers? They were not soldiers or pirates; they followed a profession with zeal, but were not missionaries, doctors, or spies. They had a different purpose, a very dangerous mission. They risked their lives to find something seemingly ordinary: plants.

The occupation of plant hunting has existed for at least thirty-five centuries, ever since Queen Hatshepsut of ancient Egypt dispatched a convoy of men on ships to bring back frankincense trees from the African land of Punt. Throughout history, plant hunting has been part of the

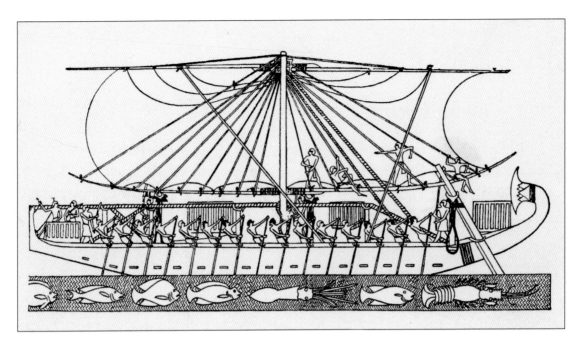

The first recorded plant-hunting expedition: a ship heading to Punt and tree saplings being loaded for Queen Hatshepsut. Line drawings from Amelia Edwards's *Pharaohs, Fellahs, and Explorers* (Harper 1892).

motivation behind important events. Because of President Thomas Jefferson's interest in botany, he dispatched Meriwether Lewis and William Clark to travel across America to catalog and study all the species of plants they could locate; they found dozens of exciting new items—bear grass, false buckthorn, green rabbitbrush, Jacob's ladder, Lewis's monkey flower, and western red cedar. While on an expedition with Captain James

Cook in 1770, Sir Joseph Banks discovered many new species in Australia and New Zealand. And the sailors on the HMS *Bounty,* who in 1789 organized a mutiny against their captain, William Bligh, were particularly annoyed at having to leave Tahiti in order to get exotic breadfruit plants safely to England. These outraged seamen dropped the plants over the side as part of their rebellion.

For centuries, plant hunters traveled to the far corners of the earth, gathering specimens for scientists, botanical gardens, and government agencies. As was said of one of them: "The mere suspicion of a plant unknown to him was an irresistible attraction. He thought nothing of scaling almost inaccessible mountains and both risked his life and ruined his health by his excursions."

Sir Joseph Banks of England—who not only searched for plants around the world himself but sent many other botanical travelers into the field—warned potential researchers that plant hunting would expose them to "extremes of heat or cold, hunger and thirst, tropical fevers and contact with revolting diseases and creatures, shipwreck and sudden death."

Some plant hunters—such as Baron Alexander von Humboldt and Sir Joseph Dalton Hooker—came from the wealthy, privileged class. But many who took up the profession—Frank Meyer, Joseph Rock, and Ynés Mexía—gathered plants to make a living, often being paid just a few cents for each specimen. The hunters found valuable medicinal plants, such as the cinchona tree, which produced quinine for treating malaria. They transported plant species such as rubber trees from one geographic area to another, where they became important commercial crops. With superhuman efforts, collectors gathered species from all over the earth and brought them back to their own countries. These heroic men and women, often seized by what they called "botanomania," lived—and even died—because of their passion for plants.

CHAPTER 1

THE INDIANA JONES OF THE NINETEENTH CENTURY

I walked along the beach to observe a group of crocodiles asleep in the sun, their tails, covered with broad scaly plates, resting on each other. Small herons, as white as snow, walked on their backs, even on their heads, as if they were tree trunks . . . As I looked in that direction I saw [a tiger] lying down under the thick foliage . . . eighty steps away from me. Never had a tiger seemed so enormous . . . I carried on walking, without breaking into a run or moving my arms . . . The further away I got the more I quickened my pace. I was so tempted to turn round and see if the cat was chasing me! Luckily I resisted the impulse, and the tiger remained lying down.

—Alexander von Humboldt

IN THESE WORDS, Baron Alexander von Humboldt recorded one of many near-death experiences he had while exploring uncharted regions of Venezuela and Brazil in 1800. For several months, Humboldt, who came from a wealthy German family, and his traveling companion, Pierre Bonpland from France, had been thrilled by the sights, smells, noises, animals, and plants of the area. As they traveled, they sketched, took extensive notes, and gathered specimens. Well supplied with equipment, they brought with them forty-two advanced scientific instruments: microscopes and telescopes, thermometers and barometers, a rain gauge, quadrants and sextants, a Leyden jar for storing static electricity, a magnetic needle, a galvanometer to measure electric currents, and a pendulum. They even carried an instrument that compared degrees of blueness in the colors of the sky.

Although he had traveled throughout much of Europe, Humboldt marveled at the plants in this part of the world. "What magnificent vegetation!" he wrote. "Cocoa-nut palms from fifty to sixty feet in height . . . bananas, and a host of trees with enormous leaves and sweet-smelling flowers as large as one's hand, all of which are entirely new . . . How brilliant the plumage of birds and the colours of the fishes!—even the crabs are sky-blue and gold!" In his journals, published in 1814 as *Personal Narrative of a Journey to the Equinoctial Regions of the New Continent*, he described in detail the breathtaking plant and animal life he discovered.

Oil painting of Alexander von Humboldt in 1809 by Friedrich Georg Weitsch.

But the joys of this journey were definitely tempered by tremendous challenges. Humboldt was stalked by jaguars (a type of South American tiger), tormented by insects, threatened by crocodiles, and abandoned by his guides. He narrowly escaped being poisoned. Yet even these terrifying events did not diminish his enthusiasm for his mission.

The rain forests of Venezuela, one of the first habitats that Humboldt saw in South America, contained over five million botanical and animal

Watercolor of Mount Chimboazo, one of the sights that Alexander von Humboldt viewed while in South America. From the book *Vues des Cordillères, et monumens des peoples indigènes de l'Amérique.*

species; in fact 15 percent of the world's plants are found there. These jungles stretched out like an ocean. Gigantic trees rose from the ravines. Their black bark, burned by the sun, contrasted with the thick green carpet of climbing vines, called lianas, that covered them. Orchids blanketed the trunks; lianas stretched from one tree to another, a hundred feet in the air. Humboldt marveled at the smell of the thick jungles—a tantalizing mixture of the aromas of flowers, fruits, and even the tree wood itself.

After exploring the forests, Humboldt and Bonpland, traveling in a boat piloted by native guides, headed down the Orinoco River, which flows into the Amazon. In the boat's large cabin, covered with leaves to shelter them from sun and rain, they placed their equipment and provisions for the coming month—oranges, tamarinds, bananas, eggs, and chocolate. The baron also brought along a large mastiff, called simply "the dog," for companionship. As they traveled, they added specimens to what quickly became a floating zoo, which included several primates, ranging in size from small squirrel monkeys to a large woolly one (now called Humboldt's woolly monkey), and two dozen caged birds (a macaw with purple feathers, other parrots, two cock-of-the-rocks, and a beautiful toucan, a bird of unusual intelligence). The zoo kept the boat lively; when it rained, the toucan tried to fly and the monkeys attempted to hide.

During the day, as they floated down the river, Humboldt observed an enormous number of wild animals. In the leafy treetops, howler monkeys traveled in packs of thirty or forty, creating a constant racket. In a kind of dance or ballet, they moved slowly from one high branch to another—every monkey in the group repeating the last action of the monkey before it. Jaguars appeared at the water's edge, drinking from the river and then eventually disappearing back into the jungle. Other animals emerged, one

This map of New Spain was drawn by Alexander von Humboldt. He left a version of it in Washington, D.C., when he visited President Thomas Jefferson in 1804.

after another—American panthers, magnificent black pheasants, flamingos, pink pelicans, spoonbills, and herons. Crocodiles, often in large groups, stretched out on sandbars. Capybaras, large rodents that could swim, lived in herds of up to sixty and became food for the predators. Humboldt found this scene to be "like paradise."

Every night when they established a camp, they placed the birds, animals, and instruments in the center, arranged hammocks for sleeping next to them, and built a fire ring on the outside to scare off jaguars. One full-moon night, the jungle vibrated with such raucous animal noises that sleep was impossible. Jaguars, pumas, sloths, and howler monkeys created a deafening roar. When jaguars approached the camp, the giant mastiff—who had been barking all night in response to the symphony of sounds—retreated under Humboldt's hammock.

But of all the Amazon's predators, nothing proved more lethal to the travelers than its insects. The men were constantly attacked by mosquitoes, large and small gnats, and tiny venomous flies. These pests caused the baron's hands to swell, making it difficult for him to do what he had come to do: harvest plants. Completely miserable, the baron wrote: "However much you try to observe the object you are studying, the mosquitoes . . . will tear you away as they cover your head and hands, pricking you with their needle-like suckers through your clothes, and climbing into your nose and mouth, making you cough and sneeze whenever you try to talk." To counteract the insects, the baron buried himself in dirt, slept in trees, rubbed his body with crocodile fat and turtle-egg oil, and slapped at the attackers—all to no avail.

Preserving plant species under these conditions proved daunting. However, the baron and Bonpland learned that the natives lived in small *hornitos*, or ovens, "small spaces without doors or windows, which they slide into on their bellies through a low opening." Inside these dwellings, a fire of green unseasoned wood, which gives off plenty of smoke, expelled all the insects. The men put these *hornitos* to use. Bonpland spent many hours in them, pressing and drying the plant specimens that they gathered daily.

While Bonpland baked himself and the plants in the *hornitos*, Humboldt wrote in his journal, making notes on the location of plants and drawing detailed pictures of the impressive vegetation all around him. He marveled at the *zamang*, the rain tree. The branches extended like an enormous umbrella, providing a home for the multitude of plants that lived on them. At another spot, he noted the cow tree, sometimes called the milk tree, whose sap provided a nourishing substance for those living around it. He discovered some beautiful Malabar chestnuts covered with enormous purple flowers, a rare long-leafed bamboo plant that grew sixty feet high, and a Brazil nut tree that could have been five to eight hundred years old. When the Brazil nut's fruit ripened in May, the huge balls, each containing fifteen

Noix exotiques.

1. Lecythis ollaria. 2. Carya olivæformis. 3. Bertholetia excelsa. 4. Pistacia Lentiscus. 5. Caryocar butyrosum. 6. Arachis hypogæa. 7. Anacardium occidentale. 8. Carya alba.

A page showing various nuts, including the large Brazil nut. From *La Belgique Horticole*, Volume VI, 1856.

Watercolor of South American landscape viewed by Humboldt and Bonpland. From *Vues des Cordillères, et monumens des peoples indigènes de l'Amérique.*

to twenty-two nuts, crashed onto the ground. Then monkeys, squirrels, and parrots rushed to the spot to fight over the prized booty.

To provide food along the way, Humboldt's guides often fished for a tasty little item that they called the *caribe*, known in English as the piranha, the most ferocious, bloodthirsty fish in the world. Related to the catfish,

the piranha inflicts incredible damage with its sharp, interlocking teeth. A school of piranhas can strip a carcass in a minute; piranhas also habitually attack things much larger than themselves.

Crocodiles and snakes also infested the river. At one point, a violent gust of wind swamped the boat with so much water that it looked like it might sink. The guides jumped overboard and swam away. But the baron was not a strong swimmer. Fortunately, his good friend Bonpland remained loyal and tried to help Humboldt swim to shore— more than a mile away. As they moved slowly in the water, they could spot at least a dozen crocodiles. "Even if we had gained the shore against the fury of the waves and the voracity of the crocodiles, we should infallibly either have perished from hunger or been torn to pieces by the tigers," Humboldt later wrote. But after struggling in the water, they realized that the same gusts of wind that had threatened to sink their boat now filled its sails again. With great effort, Humboldt and Bonpland managed to climb back into the boat and maneuver it to shore. Although the guides later returned to the vessel, many valuable plant specimens had been lost, carried away by the river.

In the town of Esmeralda, on the Orinoco River, the baron stopped to research one of the most infamous products of the region—nerve poison, or black curare, generated from local plants and used by the Tikuna tribe on the tips of lethal arrows. This poison kills a bird in two or three minutes and a pig in twelve; it is also quite capable of killing a human being.

When it enters a person's bloodstream, the victim becomes nauseous, vomits, and is tortured by thirst.

Humboldt watched the tribe members use clay boilers to create the poison that "kills silently, without the victim knowing where it comes from." He tasted the bitter concoction without any ill effect—as the poison only proves fatal when it pierces the skin. But his travels almost came to a tragic end when a jar of the curare accidentally spilled on his clothes. Some seeped into a sock, which he began to pull over his foot. Since he had bleeding sores from insect bites all over his feet, this chance encounter with the black curare would have killed him. Luckily he discovered the spilled poison in time.

Returning to Cumaná, Venezuela, Humboldt and Bonpland both suffered from violent fevers. At one point, Humboldt feared that Bonpland had died, only to discover that he had merely fainted. Slowly, over time, both men recovered.

With so many near-death experiences, the baron's journey reads like an escapade of Indiana Jones or some other action hero. But when it came to plant hunting, Humboldt was just your typical, ordinary collector. Many who came after him had just as amazing escapades.

CHAPTER 2

WHY DID THEY DO IT?

WHY DID THESE ADVENTUROUS SOULS, like Baron von Humboldt, willingly face crocodiles, piranhas, and jaguars just to bring home seeds, leaves, and flowers? Examine any plant. It is stationary. It appears uncomplicated, even boring. It doesn't walk or speak. Yet in pursuit of these seemingly placid objects, every plant hunter faced extraordinary danger.

Although they came from different countries and different backgrounds, most plant hunters shared similar characteristics. They loved being outdoors in the natural world. They enjoyed traveling to places often unseen by others, and they found alien landscapes mysterious and beautiful. Sometimes a passion for travel gripped them, as if they were migratory birds. In great physical shape, capable of walking and climbing long distances, they all possessed stamina, endurance, and perseverance. They chose lives that offered little physical comfort. Often they gained mastery of several languages, because they needed to negotiate with people in South America, China, Mongolia, or Turkistan. All enjoyed extended periods of being and traveling alone. Plant hunting required a temperament that flourished in isolation.

As an occupation, plant hunting strongly favored male collectors who could easily leave their homes and travel around the world by themselves;

however, over the years a few determined women made their mark in the field. From the age of six, Alice Eastwood (1859–1953) had been a plant enthusiast, having been introduced to botany by her uncle. In her twenties, she organized the herbarium of the California Academy of Sciences in San Francisco. Traveling in the Yukon for Harvard University at the age of fifty-five to study the plants of this cold region, Eastwood adapted to living in a rough cabin with a defective woodstove, a floor covered with ice, and insufficient provisions. But, she wrote, "I don't mind anything when I want to get something."

Plant hunters needed translators in many of the places they traveled. Frank Meyer with his Chinese interpreter, Chow-hai Ting. Gelatin silver-process photograph on paper.

Ynés Mexía (1870–1938) did not even experience her first plant-hunting expedition until she had turned fifty-five. She then made multiple expeditions to Central and South America, where she used her ability to speak Spanish to gain access to areas unexplored by others. Mexía wrote that she finally found in her later life "a task where I could be useful . . . while living out among the flowers."

Most plant hunters wanted to make scientific discoveries. They were inspired by the life and work of the Swedish scientist Carl Linnaeus (1707–1778), the father of modern botany, the scientific study of plants. As a young boy, the son of a pastor in a small Swedish village, Linnaeus faced poverty and hunger. He often had to patch his shoes because he could not afford better ones. Known as "the little botanist" from the age of eight, Linnaeus also became obsessed with making lists. He initially created a list of his toys; later he would make lists of cows. His need to organize and arrange his world became one of his defining characteristics—and eventually it helped make him famous.

With support from his community, Linnaeus managed to attend the University of Uppsala to pursue a degree in botany, a discipline then in the forefront of the scientific revolution. Even before he had graduated, Linnaeus—dressed in leather trousers, knee-high boots, and a hat with netting—journeyed one hundred miles, with only crude maps, in Sweden's rugged Lapland region to gather plants.

While publishing his scientific notes from that trip, Linnaeus began to develop a new system of classification for plants. At that time, different scientists named and identified plants according to their own concepts. Linnaeus believed that a universally accepted classification grid would make the exchange of scientific information easier. Returning home with no less than one hundred previously unknown species, he published his own ideas about plant classification, building on work that had already been done by John Ray of England and Joseph Tournefort of

France. Based on the concept that species should be grouped together because they shared physical characteristics, Linnaeus's system, with some changes, still forms the basis of all scientific classification today. It was simple, logical, and easy to understand, and it could be mastered quickly.

Linnaeus divided the natural world into three kingdoms: animal, vegetable, and mineral. He then added other qualifiers—phylum, class, order, genus, and species. As he named everything from buffaloes to buttercups, he began to create order out of the natural world, or, as his motto has been translated, "God created. Linnaeus organized."

Every living creature was given a descriptive Latin name. Each name was short, unique, and standardized. It began with the genus (general family name) and was followed by the species (a unique name). Just as humans had a family name, Smith or Jones, and a personal name, John or Juanita, plants and animals would have similar names in Latin. Human beings became *Homo sapiens* under this system, household cats *Felis catus,* and the common daisy *Bellis perennis.* Lions and tigers, members of the same family, became *Panthera leo* and *Panthera tigris.*

This system provided for all creatures a unique name that could be universally adopted. The common dog rose, for instance, had been called *Rosa sylvestris inodora seu canina* by some scientists and *Rosa sylvestris alba cum rubore, folio glabro* by others. Linnaeus renamed it *Rosa* (the genus) *canina* (the species). Information could now be communicated easily from one scientist to another, no matter where they lived or what language they spoke.

After Linnaeus established this universal system of plant classification, hundreds of his students, whom he called "apostles," searched the far corners of the earth to find previously unidentified species to fit into his classification grid. Other plant hunters worked for universities and acquired species that could be studied, classified, cataloged, and given distinct names. Some gathered species for the impressive formal gardens located

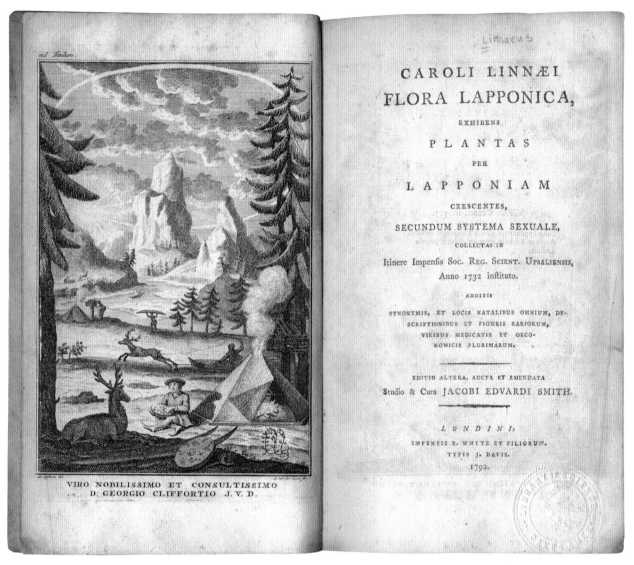

The opening pages of Carl Linnaeus's *Flora Lapponica*.

throughout Europe. The most important of these, Kew Gardens in England (now the Royal Botanic Gardens), began as the exotic garden of Lord Capel of Tewkesbury and was slowly enriched by British monarchs. From the 1700s through the 1900s, thousands of plant hunters scoured the planet to increase its vast botanic collection.

If a plant hunter located a new species, the plant might be named after

Drawing of various fungi from Linnaeus's *Flora Lapponica*.

him or her, giving scientific travelers a chance to claim a bit of immortality for themselves and make a permanent imprint on science. Ynés Mexía admitted that she longed to find new species that would become "permanent exhibits under my name in the Herbaria of the world for all time to come." So the plant *Mimosa mexiae* bears her name, as does *Mexianthus mexicanus*, a member of an entirely new genus that she located in the Mexican state of Jalisco.

Besides being part of the ongoing scientific study of plants, many hunters discovered that they could make a living by traveling around in the natural world, something they enjoyed doing anyway. John Bartram (1699–1777) of Philadelphia spent forty years hunting plants in North America. One day, he discovered a beautiful patch of birdfoot violets. He dreamed of them the following night. When he woke the next morning, he decided to devote himself to the study of plants. Fortunately, Peter Collinson, a London merchant, agreed to pay for plant species from America. Taking few possessions on his trips—a bedroll, books, plant-collecting tools, and firearms—Bartram ate only berries, nuts, fruits, and wild game. On his trip through the Carolinas, Georgia, and Florida, he kept a diary, and his maps contain descriptive names—"Impenetrable," "Endless Mountains," and "Dismal Vale." But even though the landscape proved daunting, his love of what he was doing, and the money to be gained from selling plants, always kept him searching for unusual specimens.

The Scotsman David Douglas (1799–1834) discovered at an early age that he wanted to become a botanical traveler. The son of a stonemason, Douglas had little use for school and left before he turned ten, not planning to return. Then he was apprenticed to a head gardener at Scone Palace in Scotland—who worked magic on the young boy. Or the plants did. In his seven-year apprenticeship, Douglas discovered that he wanted to be not only a botanist, but also a plant hunter.

In 1824, England's Horticultural Society began sending Douglas on several expeditions to the United States to locate species not currently found in England and Europe. Arriving at the mouth of the Columbia River on what is now the state border between Washington and Oregon, he set out to explore the wild and untraveled Pacific Northwest. One of the spots he visited bore the name Cape Disappointment. But Douglas rarely allowed either the extremely challenging terrain or what it was named deter him.

While in this area, he became obsessed with finding a single species, the elusive sugar pine. After observing Kalapooia tribe members in the Multnomah River area chewing large, sweet pine seeds, he became eager to find the trees that produced them, which he named *Pinus lambertiana*. Douglas attached himself to a party of fur hunters heading into the region where he believed the pines to be located. Although the rest of the group rode, Douglas always walked, using his horse only to carry his baggage.

A portrait of David Douglas, who hunted plants in the United States for Kew Gardens. Created by Daniel Macnee in 1828 with colored chalk on paper.

This made it easier for him to collect seeds, including some from the headache tree (*Umbellularia californica*), so named because its leaves, when crushed and sniffed, caused a splitting headache lasting about half an hour. After a grizzly bear treed and injured one member of the party, the fur hunters decided to stop in a small town. Not Douglas. He wanted those seeds!

Traveling on by himself, he suddenly toppled into a deep gulley. There he lay unconscious for five hours until members of the Kalapooia tribe found him. His foot was seriously injured. Because he was in such pain, he sliced open his own wound, let blood run out of it, and then bathed his foot in ice-cold water. Fortunately, this self-cure worked. Douglas then continued his journey—drenched and frozen, racked with head pain, seized by belly cramps, and plagued by dizzy spells.

After some thirteen miles by himself, Douglas came upon a tribe member who pointed him in the direction of the pines, a long twenty miles ahead. When Douglas finally reached his destination, he looked up in amazement. The trees towered above him, rising as high as 215 feet in the air.

To harvest the pine cones at the top of these tall beauties, he had to shoot them down with his rifle. As he blasted away, he found himself surrounded by a war party that looked decidedly unfriendly. Fortunately, they merely wanted tobacco. Douglas gladly promised to give it to them if they would gather the sugar pine cones. They agreed, and he headed back

Watercolor of the *Pinus lambertiana*. From Aylmer Bourke Lambert's *Description of the Genus Pinus*.

Pinus Lambertiana.

to civilization, famished and tired, with his prized harvest. Although Douglas is best remembered for the first tree that he discovered in North America, the Douglas fir, he was particularly proud of these sugar pines—*Pinus lambertiana*—because he had gone to such great lengths to find them.

Many plant hunters put their energies into searching for a useful plant, one that might help the economy of their country—just as the Douglas fir became an important part of the forestry industry in England and America. In 1800, President Thomas Jefferson wrote, "The greatest service that can be rendered any country is to add a useful plant to its culture." Dedicated plant hunters wanted to render that service, to find a plant that when introduced to their own lands would benefit all the citizens.

Working in the early 1900s for the United States Department of Agriculture, Frank Meyer declared that he wanted to "skim the earth in search of things good for man." In China, he walked a thousand miles, collecting samples of plants that might become valuable crops. He found wheat that could be planted in South Dakota and a cherry tree that adapted to the climate of California.

Most plant hunters were motivated by several things: a desire to serve science, the prospect of finding meaningful work, and a passion for plants. During the early 1900s, Ernest H. Wilson (1876–1930) traveled in China for both a nursery, James Veitch and Sons, and the Arnold Arboretum in Boston. For the latter, he promised to search for the rare regal lily in China's remote Szechuan region. In the desolate Min Valley, Wilson saw, carved in the rocks, giant Chinese characters warning of the danger of landslides. But this area harbored lilies, and he was determined to find them. There "by the wayside, in rock-crevice by the torrent's edge and high up on the mountainside and precipice," he discovered what he had been searching for, regal lilies in full bloom.

Wilson gathered over six thousand bulbs before heading back to

Passports of Ernest H. Wilson and his wife, Ellen Garderton Wilson, showing their various adventures around the globe.

civilization. As Chinese porters carried Wilson in a sedan chair, a huge boulder suddenly crashed down the hill. It struck the chair, breaking it into pieces, before it plummeted into the gorge. Wilson got up slowly. His right leg had been fractured in two places. He was three days away from any medical help. What if his guides simply decided to abandon him?

Immediately taking charge, Wilson fashioned his camera tripod as a splint for his leg so that he could keep going. But as he hobbled along a narrow track between the mountains, a train of fifty mules appeared in front of him, coming from the opposite direction. At first each member of Wilson's party tried to edge his way past the mules, but a continual stream of pebbles indicated that another avalanche might occur at any moment. What could the injured Wilson do? Desperate, he lay horizontally across the narrow track, and, one by one, fifty mules stepped over him. "Then it was that I realized the size of the mule's hoof," he later wrote. Fortunately, none landed on him.

After Wilson got through this narrow pass, his guides carried him in another chair through more hills, over miles of rough paths. Three days

Photograph of Ernest H. Wilson in western China with other plant hunters and dogs.

Photograph of Ernest H. Wilson with "reformed headhunters and armed policemen" in the mountains of Formosa in 1918. Plant hunters met people of varied backgrounds in their journeys.

later, in a bad state, Wilson arrived at a missionary station. Gangrene had settled in his leg, and the doctor announced that it should be amputated. But Wilson refused to allow an operation. Fortunately, the infection didn't spread and merely made his leg shrink in size. For the rest of his life, Wilson walked with his "lily limp" and had to wear an orthopedic boot.

In 1919, Wilson became director of Harvard's Arnold Arboretum, sending others into the field to locate rare, intriguing, and valuable plants. Often his friends asked him about the hardships he endured, traveling

Photograph of Charles Sprague Sargent and Ernest H. Wilson standing in front of a Higan cherry tree at the Arnold Arboretum, Jamaica Plain, Massachusetts.

throughout the world. He did, of course, undergo great difficulties, becoming lame as a result of his travels. But, as he wrote, he also spent each day experiencing the beauty of the natural world—savoring "the music of babbling brook, the smell of mother earth and the mixed odors of myriad flowers." Plant hunters such as Wilson traveled through rough jungles and inhospitable mountains because their work allowed them to spend their days in the outdoor world that they loved.

CHAPTER 3

BRINGING THE PLANTS HOME ALIVE

THE PLANT HUNTERS braved many dangers, but the plants themselves also faced multiple risks before they arrived at their final destinations. Many of our common American plants are immigrants. Daffodils, tulips, and hyacinths originated in the Eastern Mediterranean; geraniums in South Africa; many exotic orchids and begonias in South America; flowering cherry and crabapple trees in Asia. But before they could grow here, they had to be harvested successfully and then transported with great care. Millions of plants died as they were taken from one country to another. But plant hunters struggled to keep enough alive so that some of them could grow and thrive. How did they manage?

Before searching for specimens, plant hunters needed to assemble their plant-harvesting equipment: scissors, a variety of knives (including a pen knife and a bowie knife), a magnifying glass, a trowel, gloves, labels, tweezers, razors, thin glass, and cotton wool or lint. Sometimes a plant hunter would carry a vasculum—a botanist's box for storing plants, commonly made of sheet metal with a hinged lid and a shoulder strap. He or she would also bring a portable plant press and special papers on which to dry one example of each specimen as a scientific record.

Once a plant hunter arrived in an area, he or she had to locate a guide and sometimes a translator who could speak the language of the native

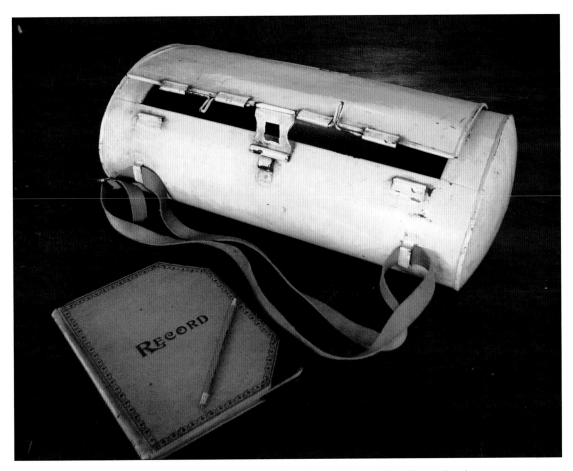

Photograph of vasculum with the notebook of explorer Ernest H. Wilson, both in possession of the Arnold Arboretum.

people. Usually the botanist set off with a small group. But an exploration party could be any size. Joseph Dalton Hooker, whose expedition to India in 1847 was financed by the British government, found safety in numbers. Trained from childhood to be a scientist by his father (William Jackson Hooker, who became director of Kew Gardens), Hooker sought live plants for his father to grow at Kew. Determined to please his father as well as his government, Hooker left nothing to chance. He assembled a group of fifty-five people that included a personal servant, a chief plant collector, an interpreter, natives to harvest multiple species, and porters to carry

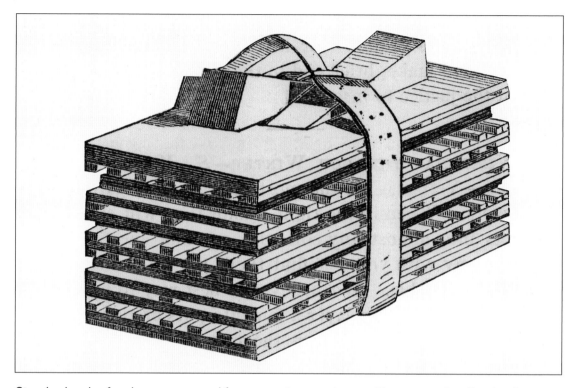

Simple sketch of a plant press, used for preserving specimens. First printed in *Gardner's Monthly*.

tents, bedding, and provisions—lots of provisions. Hooker brought canned meats, cases of salmon, and brandy; he always carried enough food to serve several elegant banquets. For scientific equipment, Hooker carried a chronometer, a telescope, a compass, barometers, and a sextant. He even transported a solid-oak traveling desk!

To protect his enormous convoy, Hooker hired an escort of five Nepalese sepoys (guards armed with knives and swords), who looked quite impressive in their scarlet jackets and skullcaps. With so many colorful characters, the assembled group could have been the cast of a Hollywood extravaganza. But even though Hooker surrounded himself with guards, he rarely got a good night's sleep. The yaks that carried all this equipment turned out to be inquisitive insomniacs; they constantly poked their heads into Hooker's tent and snorted at him until he awoke! Still, Hooker discovered that even the wild animals surrounding him could be useful—elephants, for example, could be trained to harvest plants in the high trees with their trunks.

Whether they traveled in groups or solo, all plant hunters had to establish a schedule far away from civilization. Like most of them, Hooker awoke early, at four or five in the morning. After breakfast, he made sure that everything had been carefully packed to travel. Then he left the camp by ten and set out searching for plants. Because of the danger to both men

Portrait of Joseph Dalton Hooker. Lithograph by J. H. Maguire created in 1851.

Sketch of a typical suspension bridge in the Khasia Hills, India, similar to the ones that frightened Joseph Hooker. From his *Himalayan Journals*.

and animals, he did not want his party traveling at night. Generally, he stopped to establish his next camp between four and six in the afternoon. Then, while his dinner was being prepared, he would press plants, make sketches, and write up his findings for the day. By ten, after working sixteen to eighteen hours, he finally went to bed.

But when Hooker took his party into the Himalayas, he found that his schedule completely fell apart. At the height of thirteen thousand feet, he suffered from the "lassitude, headache, and giddiness" of altitude sickness and had to take shelter in a stone hut. At fifteen thousand feet, he had "no strength to crawl farther . . . [and had] never felt more ill" in his life. He decided to take his scientific notes while climbing up the terrain in the morning, because when he came down later in the day he was always sick. Normally stoic, Hooker found it difficult to keep steady "under the aggravations of pain in the forehead, lassitude, oppression of breathing," all made more intense by "a dense drizzling fog, a keen wind, a slippery footing, which I was stumbling at every few steps, and ice-cold wet feet, hands, and eyelids."

For Hooker as well as other plant hunters, the records kept of the travels, including descriptions of the plants discovered during the day, were critical for each mission. It was important to attach these notes to a map of the area, so that another scientist might locate the same tree or group of plants in the future. After the invention of the camera in the 1800s, plant hunters began to travel with them to visually record their discoveries. Before cameras, they took great care to create accurate sketches. Many had taken drawing lessons as part of their scientific training; some, such as Joseph Hooker, were actually skilled artists and painters.

Besides using a drawing or photograph, they also wanted to preserve a full specimen of the plant. Although ideally the best specimen would include all parts of a plant—bud, flower, fruit, roots, stem, and leaves—most often some of these (bud, flower, and fruit) emerged at different times in a plant's life cycle, making it impossible to preserve them all at once. The botanist had to harvest, carefully, as much of the plant as he or she could find and then run the specimen through a plant field press, using either a special paper or sometimes newspaper to help blot and dry it. While doing this, the plant hunter needed to make sure that the shape of the plant was preserved, not distorted.

Finally, the plant hunter needed to survey all the living materials that had been gathered and find ways to pack and store everything. Several different parts of a plant can be used to reproduce it—a bud, cutting, division or section, bulb, rhizome (an underground stem), runner, or seed. All

Kangchenjunga from Singtam, the Himalayan countryside. Lithograph created by Walter Hood Fitch in the 1850s for Joseph Hooker's *Himalayan Journals.*

these parts of the plant serve as germplasm—the plant's genetic resources, which can be used to duplicate it.

Seeds, essentially the eggs of the flowering plant, contain all the parts of a plant in a protective coating. Some seeds are as fine as dust, others as large as cannon balls; some have odd shapes, like parasols or fans. Some seeds have a very short life span, while others can last for years. Grain sealed in the Egyptian pyramids can still germinate and create a new plant even after thousands of years. Seeds are the most easily transplanted part of the plant and weigh the least. But they are not fail-safe as a means of reproducing the plant.

Out of the thousands of seeds Joseph Hooker sent back to Kew Gardens from India, only a few actually germinated and produced plants. He tried various methods of preserving seeds—he packed them in cans, wrapped them in oilcloth, sent them in paper packets, and even enclosed them in letters. But far too often they were ruined by water or eaten by insects before they arrived.

Transporting living plant stock could be even more difficult. It might be weeks or months from when the plant was harvested in the field to when the botanist arrived in a port city. During that time, the stock would be carried by mules or horses, sent on flimsy boats down rivers, and exposed to all kinds of weather and temperature changes. Basically, from the moment the plant was harvested, its fate was uncertain. It was much more likely to perish than survive. Because plant hunters wanted to ensure that at least some specimens might survive, they collected large numbers of each plant, often destroying a good part of the landscape in the process. Joseph Hooker's workers would cut down entire trees just to secure the orchids living at the top of them. Ten thousand trees might die before they gathered four thousand orchids.

While a plant hunter's quest ended with the delivery of the plant material to a port city and a ship, his anxieties did not. He needed to find a way

Rhododendron dahlousie, which Joseph Dalton Hooker believed to be the most beautiful of his discoveries. From *The Rhododendrons of the Sikkim-Himalaya*.

to package his still-living plants so that they could survive a long ocean voyage. If sea spray got into the cases, it could cause the plants to ferment and quickly destroy them. For the plants to survive, the case lids had to be lifted from time to time to provide fresh air, and often sailors forgot to do this. The rats that inhabited ships ate through boxes of plants, while insects could easily devour every living plant on board. Heat, humidity, or exceedingly dry air could also be the kiss of death for these plants. And if a heavy storm hit the ship, the plant consignment was often the first thing crews jettisoned into the sea to make the boat more stable.

In fact, little progress had been made in the transporting of plants for several thousand years. But in 1829, Dr. Nathaniel Bagshaw Ward, a physician with a passion for botany, accidentally discovered how he could preserve plants by growing them in bottles. One day, Ward left a caterpillar and some soil in a glass jar. When he returned later, he found a small fern growing in the bottom of the jar, one that had sprouted from a seed buried in the soil. Ward then had a carpenter build a closely fitted wooden case, covered with glazed glass. Essentially, it resembled a fish tank for plants, with a top over it.

In these cases, he successfully shipped fragile ferns and grasses from England to New South Wales, Australia, and then published a book about his experiments with these portable greenhouses. These cases provided a

Early examples of the Wardian case. From Nathaniel Ward's *On the Growth of Plants*.

Hand-colored lithograph of *Rhododendron barbatum* by Walter Hood Fitch. From *The Rhododendrons of Sikkim-Himalaya.*

weatherproof way to transport plants over long ocean voyages and keep them healthy. As the first scientist to use the Wardian case, Joseph Hooker successfully shipped many living plants to Kew Gardens. With this new scientific discovery, he transported thousands of rhododendrons from India to England.

On occasion, the plant hunter would travel back to his or her native country with the treasured plants. Usually, however, he or she headed out on a new expedition, spending months or even years in challenging new terrain, learning a language other than his or her native tongue, living away from family and friends—eager to discover more plants.

CHAPTER 4

BRINGING THEMSELVES HOME ALIVE

EVEN AS PLANT HUNTERS worked to make sure that their specimens thrived, they had no guarantees that they themselves would survive. The threats to their lives came daily, often from unexpected enemies. Some of their problems resulted from the natural world itself. They traveled in unfamiliar areas, often over difficult terrain, with very sketchy maps, not even sure if they could find food and water. Wild animals stalked them; insects plagued them. Sometimes other human beings threatened to rob or kill these itinerant scientists. Like all adventurers and wilderness explorers, those who lived to tell their stories had cheated death many times.

In 1874, the English botanist W. E. P. Giles was exploring the vast deserts of central Australia. Setting out with his hunting partner from a base camp at Fort McKellar, he discovered a leak in one of his large water bags. The two men decided to continue, even though the temperature had already climbed to 96 degrees Fahrenheit. Camping that night, they hung their remaining bags of water in a tree to protect them. But one of their horses attacked a bag with her teeth—spraying the water all over the ground. Now neither the men nor the animals had enough water.

Giles decided to send his partner back to Fort McKellar with the horses for more water. But a few hours later, he began to realize the danger he

TAMBUR RIVER AT THE LOWER LIMIT OF FIRS.

The landscape seen by Joseph Dalton Hooker in India. From *Himalayan Journals*.

had put himself in. He now stood sixty miles from the closest oasis, and eighty miles from Fort McKellar. If his partner failed to return in five or six days, Giles would most likely die of thirst. So strapping what little remaining water he had onto his back, he began to walk in the direction of the oasis. Even trudging through the desert into the night, he could travel at most five miles each day. Within a few days, he became dehydrated and dizzy; when he stood up, his head would swim. Frequently he thought he would simply die, alone and away from civilization. Then, miraculously, after walking for almost two weeks without a map, Giles saw the oasis! He drank, rested, refilled his water keg—and then continued walking. Three days later, he finally staggered into Fort McKellar, only to learn, to his horror, that his partner had died in the desert and had never reached the fort.

Just as the terrain itself could

challenge explorers, wild animals—grizzly bears, cougars, vampire bats—made travel potentially lethal for anyone who went into wilderness areas. Richard Spruce, who traveled in the Amazon for Kew Gardens from 1849 through 1864, wrote chilling accounts of the problems caused by the creatures, large and small, that he encountered. In one of his living spaces, he was plagued by sauba ants, termites, scorpions, and cockroaches. The ants drove him particularly wild, because they attacked and carried off his plant specimens. He "burned them, smoked them, drowned them, trod on them," but the ants would always come back. Termites even ate his towel! But the vampire bats of the area became his most terrifying enemy.

A photograph of Richard Spruce taken in the 1860s.

When Spruce entered one house where he hoped to live and work, he found "large patches of dried-up blood on the floor which had been drawn from my predecessors by those midnight blood-letters." Spruce discovered that the bats "do not stop at the toes, but bite occasionally on the legs, fingers' end, nose, and chin and forehead."

In the end, however, even the plants themselves could be dangerous. William Colenso, who collected in Australia in the 1840s, had the dubious honor of having a dangerous plant, *Aciphylla colensoi*, named after him. This plant, he said, looked like a fixed bayonet; it drew blood from every member of his plant-hunting party. "Imagine a living circle of five feet diameter . . . with all its many harsh spiny ray-like leaves radiating alike outwardly from its carrot-shaped root, forming almost a plane of living elastic spears, composed of sharp and still points, or flat spikes, each several inches long." One of the party, enraged by the damage the plant caused, took an ax to it, but he had to abandon even that approach because the plant seemed to be winning the battle—pricking him, causing blood to spurt. Others who tried to harvest the plant referred to it as "infernal."

But if the natural world could be inhospitable, so could the humans who inhabited these places. Being robbed by bandits was a constant fear of many plant hunters, because they were often traveling either alone or in a small group. Benedict Roezl from Bohemia (now part of the Czech Republic), the most stalwart of the orchid hunters who traveled throughout Mexico and South America in the 1870s, appears to have been particularly prone to encountering bandits; he was held up and robbed seventeen times! At one point, his assailants got so exasperated by his lack of possessions (he traveled merely with some clothes, a horse, and bundles and bundles of plants) that they seemed on the verge of killing him. They pulled out their knives to cut his throat. But the leader of the group held up his hand. Could the weed collector be a lunatic? Or was he just a crazed holy man wandering the countryside gathering flowers? It would be bad luck to kill a holy man. So they let him go—and rode off to find another victim.

During the early 1900s, George Forrest traveled in China's Hunan Province for the Edinburgh Botanic Garden in Scotland, searching for exotic plants. On one of his trips, he set out for a remote area near the Tibetan border and walked into a volatile political situation. A member of a British expedition had invaded the Tibetan holy city of Lhasa. Because of this incident, all Europeans were considered "white devils." Unaware that Tibetan guerrillas, often Buddhist monks, were attacking foreigners in

Photograph of explorer George Forrest with a canine companion; most of the explorers took dogs with them on their trips.

the area, Forrest arrived with his team at a French mission station, where he established a base for his plant collecting.

But a few weeks later, a Frenchman, half starved and half naked, crawled into the mission; he and his colleagues had been attacked and tortured by the monks. He urged everyone to leave the mission at once. The eighty people there began an immediate evacuation. By the light of a rising moon, they moved along a narrow and dangerous track near the roaring Mekong River. Unfortunately, a member of the party made a noise. Suddenly a shrill whistle pierced the air. Forrest took a side path, to scout out what was happening. At that very moment, the Tibetan guerrillas and the party from the mission collided. Sixty-six people in the party were killed immediately, some by poison arrows.

Armed with a Winchester repeating rifle and a revolver, Forrest fled. With little sense of the countryside and the guerrillas in pursuit, he deliberately ran in circles, covering his tracks. Then he leaped off the path into a dense jungle, rolling about two hundred feet before he came to a halt. Bruised, his clothes shredded, he hid during the day and moved cautiously by night, although he could often see the torches of his enemies nearby. He decided to discard his boots because they made distinctive tracks. At one point, to foil his pursuers, he waded in an icy stream that rose up to his chest. As he dodged his enemies, he passed over hills covered with primulas, gentians, saxifrages, and lilies—some of the very plants he had been searching for. But he was in no position to linger or collect a single specimen.

"At the end of eight days I had ceased to care whether I lived or died; my feet were swollen out of all shape, my hands and face torn with thorns, and my whole person caked with mire. I was nearly dead with hunger and fatigue . . . and quite delirious," Forrest wrote later. After traveling over glaciers covered with snow, ice, and rocks that tore his feet to ribbons, he arrived in what he thought to be a safe region. But there in a maize field, he stepped on a bamboo stake, which passed between the bones of his foot. Now he was hobbled, famished, and nearly dead. Finally, he found refuge in a mission house that was protected by Chinese troops.

"I lost everything I possessed . . . with the exception of the rags I stood in, my rifle, revolver and two belts of cartridges. What was much more serious, I lost nearly all the results of a season's work, a collection of most valuable plants," about two thousand different species.

Some plant hunters, however, did not manage to foil assailants. Frank Meyer rarely spent any time in his adopted country, the United States; instead he traveled most of his adult years in the Far East as an employee of

Gelatin silver-process photograph of Frank Nicholas Meyer in Turkistan.

the United States Department of Agriculture. Meyer successfully completed three missions in China, sending home valuable crops to be planted in America, including many that still grace the American landscape. He avoided disaster a number of times. On one of his trips home he booked passage to America on the *Lusitania* rather than its competing ship, the *Titanic*, which struck an iceberg and sent 1,517 passengers to their deaths in

Gelatin silver-process photograph of Frank Nicholas Meyer in China with local workers helping him transport his supplies on a ferry.

the icy waters. But on his fourth trip to China, in 1918, while going down the Yangtze River on a boat, Meyer simply vanished, only to be found dead later. Because he traveled alone, no one knows to this day what happened to him. He paid for his passion for plants with his life—a fate that every one of these explorers accepted as a possible outcome of their occupation.

CHAPTER 5

PLANT SUPERSTARS

IN THEIR TRAVELS, the plant hunters often searched for a single plant that had tremendous value. Sometimes just one plant could make its owner extraordinarily wealthy. In the 1600s, tulips became the craze in the Netherlands—and vast fortunes were paid for rare tulips. For one prized bulb, the owner received two loads of wheat, four of rye, a thousand pounds of cheese, two barrels of butter, four oxen, eight pigs, twelve sheep, a bed, and a suit of clothes. Later, in Victorian England, orchids were so valued that some orchid sellers, such as Frederick Sandler and Son, sent dozens of plant hunters around the world to locate rare species.

Some plants were sought because they helped cure a disease—such as the bark of the cinchona tree, which helped treat malaria. Other plants might make money as a crop—like the forty-two soybean varieties that Frank Meyer gathered in Asia for the United States Department of Agriculture.

To protect extremely valuable species growing within their borders, many countries passed strict laws that made it illegal to remove them. If a special kind of tea plant was growing in China, for instance, the Chinese wanted their country to be the only source of that tea so that prices remained high. In pursuit of these superstars, plant hunters engaged in espionage and even stealing. Such was the case of Henry Alexander Wickham.

In 1876, Joseph Dalton Hooker (who followed his father to become the director of Kew Gardens) examined some sketches made by Wickham, one of the Kew plant hunters traveling in South America. These drawings indicated that Wickham had located the coveted *Hevea brasiliensis*, a superb rubber tree plant. Hooker wrote to Wickham, begging him to acquire seeds. Returning to the place where he had sketched the plants in Brazil, Wickham managed to locate the plant and harvest a valuable crop of some seventy thousand seeds. But since this plant was monitored by the Brazilian government, he decided to hide the real purpose of his trip back to England and slip these seeds, unnoticed, past Brazilian customs officials. He chartered a local steamer, the *Amazonas,* to carry what he called his "botanic collection" to London. He then enlisted the help of the

Photograph of Henry Alexander Wickham, around 1900, standing in a British rubber-tree plantation.

A typical Chinese junk, or ship. From Robert Fortune's *Three Years' Wanderings in the Northern Provinces of China.*

British consul, who asked the local customs department to quickly clear Wickham's collection of Brazilian plants that were destined for study at Kew Gardens. Everyone worked overtime to cover up the real purpose of the trip, and officials cleared Wickham's cargo without ever suspecting that it contained the rubber tree seeds.

Traveling to London with his valuable specimens, Wickham left others to unload his botanic collection when the boat docked and immediately hailed a cab to take him and his seventy thousand seeds to Kew Gardens. From these seeds, two thousand rubber trees grew and thrived in Kew.

Hooker used them to establish in Ceylon (present-day Sri Lanka) one of England's most profitable industries. No spy stealing secrets ever helped his country more than Wickham.

In the 1840s, Robert Fortune, who was traveling in China as a plant hunter for England, had a chilling experience with pirates—and then became one himself. After a short trip to the interior of the country to gather native plants, Fortune lay on the deck of a Chinese junk, weakened by fever. Suddenly, pirates appeared, bearing down on the ship. The crew panicked; they were prepared to give the pirates anything they wanted, even the plants. Not Fortune. He pulled himself up, so weak he could barely stand. Then he waited until the pirate ship came alongside the junk. Taking a double-barreled gun that had been provided by England's Royal Horticulture Society, he blasted away. The pirate ship pulled back. When it came alongside the junk again, Fortune continued firing. Beaten back again, the pirates tried one last attack—but Fortune refused to surrender and kept shooting at them. Finally, the pirates sailed away. Fortune's ship and its entire crew had been saved single-handedly by one very brave and determined botanist.

However, later Fortune became a pirate himself—in his case, a "pirate" of plants. The East India Company had located a Chinese tea plant that would adapt perfectly to the climate and terrain of India's highlands. But the Chinese fiercely protected these plants. The company asked Fortune if he could secretly collect them. Because he was already known and respected in China as a botanist, they hoped the Chinese officials might not be as suspicious of Fortune as they would be of a stranger.

For three years, Fortune gathered tea plants and seeds, placing them in Wardian cases to keep them alive. Now he carried an umbrella instead of a gun. This, of course, helped make him look eccentric rather than dangerous, even though he was pilfering one of China's most valuable crops. But Fortune did more than just collect plants. He learned valuable secrets about the growing of tea—for instance, how the same plant could be used to produce both green and black tea leaves. He also researched an intriguing rumor about harvesting tea. Local residents threw stones at monkeys in the high branches of tea plants—and the monkeys retaliated by tearing off tea branches and throwing them at the villagers. Fortune found out that the quantities of tea gathered this way was "exceedingly small" and that other, more productive ways to harvest the tea existed.

While learning everything he could about the tea industry, Fortune transferred 25,000 young plants and more than 15,000 seedlings to the foothills of the Himalayas and to Ceylon. Those plants were used to begin

"Tea Gardens at Shanghae." From Robert Fortune's *Three Years' Wanderings in the Northern Provinces of China.*

India's tea plantations, and by the end of the nineteenth century, tea had become India's largest export. Now India competed successfully with China in the tea industry.

Some plants contained medicine that could help save lives. But even these plants could be protected by the country where they originated. The disease of malaria, carried by mosquitoes, had been one of the most deadly illnesses for several centuries. In the mid-1700s, as Linnaeus cataloged all the known plants, he discovered information about a South American tree whose bark provided a cure for malaria. He named it the cinchona (or fever bark) tree. But natives in South America guarded these trees and kept them from foreigners. Many expeditions tried and failed to collect the bark and seeds of the trees.

In 1860, as director of Kew Gardens, Joseph Hooker asked Richard Spruce to locate red cinchona trees and bring back to England seeds or seedlings—anything that could be transplanted. Spruce understood a great deal about South America because he had spent fifteen years exploring the area. He set out for the Andes Mountains of Ecuador, where the trees were located. Since he couldn't get through the jungles easily, he traveled by canoe on a river made dangerous by heavy rains. When the canoe was sucked into a whirlpool, Spruce almost drowned.

Back on land, Spruce and his team searched for a trail through the dense jungle. No matter how hard they looked, they never found one. So they decided to hack their way through this sea of plants. "The rains set in with greater severity than ever—the dripping forest through which I had to push my way, soaking my garments . . . —and the mud, which even on the tops of the hills was often over the knees—made our progress very slow and painful." Spruce's health began to fail; he ran out of food; he almost drowned a second time.

Finally, he located a fine group of red cinchona trees in Limón, Ecuador. "In looking over the forest," Spruce wrote in his journal, "I could

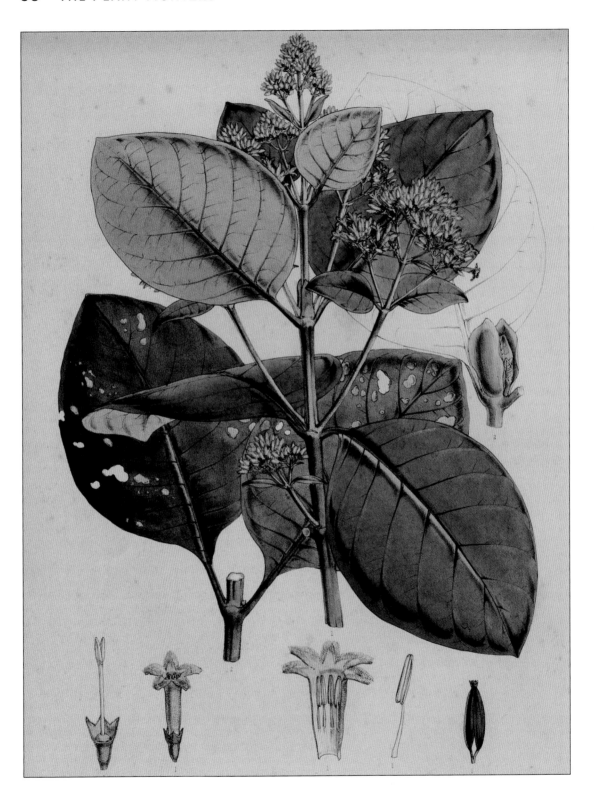

never see any other tree at all comparable to it in its beauty." Quite skilled as a negotiator, Spruce presented himself to the owners—the president of Ecuador and the Roman Catholic Church—as a scientist. He asked to secure whatever specimens grew on a very large tract of land, disguising the fact that his real goal was merely the small group of cinchona trees growing there.

Unfortunately for Spruce, Ecuador was engaged in a civil war at the time, and soldiers from both sides often visited his camp, helping themselves to provisions—even his pack mules! But Spruce remained focused on the task at hand and successfully secured a hundred thousand cinchona seeds and raised six hundred seedlings; these he packed in baskets and covered with wet moss. To protect his valuable cargo, he stretched moistened strips of calico over the baskets, hoping to keep the contents from spilling out.

Since his pack mules had been appropriated by soldiers, Spruce constructed a river raft that would allow him to travel to the nearest port. At one point, the raft was forced to go through a tangled mass of trees and branches in the middle of the river. Although the trees destroyed the small cabin on the raft, the plants survived intact. Still, Spruce worried that the seedlings were growing too fast because of the extreme heat and humidity. He needed to keep them small so that they would have a better chance of surviving the long voyage to England. Arriving at a port, he transferred these gangly specimens from rafts onto a freighter that would take them to England. Using Spruce's plants and others, the English established large cinchona plantations in Ceylon and India. Enough quinine could now be produced to treat the deadly disease of malaria around the world.

Cinchona plant from John Eliot Howard's *Illustrations of the Nueva Quinologia of Pavon*. Hand-colored plate by Walter Hood Fitch.

Joseph Dalton Hooker and Charles Darwin

It would be unfair to suggest that Joseph Dalton Hooker merely collected plants or directed the heists of valuable ones from other countries. Along with making Kew Gardens one of the foremost centers for botanical study in the world, Hooker served during the 1850s as a kind of fact-finding committee for Charles Darwin—gathering data, conducting experiments, and working out conclusions that would help Darwin develop his hypothesis about evolution. Darwin's own children, who often monitored their father's progress, would ask if he "was going to beat Dr. Hooker." Competition, however, had nothing to do with this collaboration. Not only did Hooker help Darwin with facts and research, he kept pressing Darwin to publish his views, which Hooker believed to be true from his own observations. Darwin's book turned out to be the most significant and controversial science book ever published, *On the Origin of Species.*

Darwin later referred to Hooker as one of "his two best and kindest friends." After Darwin published *On the Origin of Species*, Hooker immediately championed the new theories in the scientific community. Because Darwin claimed, among many things, that human beings were part of a long line of evolution, he became the focus of the religious wars of the nineteenth century—a battle that continues today. Journalists and creationists attacked him for undermining God and the Bible. His supporters received the same kind of abuse, and newspapers called Hooker an atheist and mocked his theology. But name-calling did not deter Hooker any more than altitude sickness in the Himalayas had; he continued to use his own intelligence and reputation to support Darwin's work.

ON

THE ORIGIN OF SPECIES

BY MEANS OF NATURAL SELECTION,

OR THE

PRESERVATION OF FAVOURED RACES IN THE STRUGGLE
FOR LIFE.

By CHARLES DARWIN, M.A.,

FELLOW OF THE ROYAL, GEOLOGICAL, LINNÆAN, ETC., SOCIETIES;
AUTHOR OF 'JOURNAL OF RESEARCHES DURING H. M. S. BEAGLE'S VOYAGE
ROUND THE WORLD.'

LONDON:
JOHN MURRAY, ALBEMARLE STREET.
1859.

First edition of *On the Origin of Species*.

Photograph of Joseph F. Rock in Tibetan dress on horseback. He traveled extensively through Indonesia, China, and Tibet.

In 1920, when Joseph F. Rock set out in the Far East to find the plant that might cure leprosy, he did not have to break any laws, but he did endure tremendous difficulties. A cure for this centuries-old disease had actually been recorded in a legend. In this tale, Rana, the king of the ancient city Benares (now called Varanasi), was afflicted with leprosy and was cast out by his people. Hiding in the jungle, Rana lived in a hollowed-out kalaw tree. Then, after eating the tree's fruit, he was cured of his dread disease. Although this story sounded like a fanciful tale, in the markets of India a foul-smelling oil, called *chaulmoogra* and pressed from kalaw fruit, *did* contain a substance that helped hold the disease of leprosy in check. If a plantation of kalaw trees could be grown, it would be a breakthrough in the treatment of this terrible disease. But, first, someone had to locate these elusive kalaw trees.

Working for the United States Department of Agriculture, Rock attempted to find these trees, scientifically named *Taraktogenos kurzii*. Traveling to Bangkok—where he believed he might locate Kalaw trees—Rock began to follow a series of leads that took him on a 350-mile trek across Indonesia. But this trip failed to produce any trees. After an arduous mountain climb, he located a single tree, not the exact species that he had been asked to find, but a close relative. He managed to gather 170 seeds— even though he had to fight off both monkeys and porcupines, who loved eating the fruit of the tree!

Following more rumors and speculations about possible tree locations, Rock arrived at an isolated village, covered with dust several feet thick. Here he discovered a colony of living kalaw trees. Villagers had lopped off

Gelatin silver-process photograph of Joseph F. Rock and a Tibetan escort party.

Rock Aceraceae specimen prepared by Joseph F. Rock for his specimen book. Plant hunters attempted to bring back one preserved specimen like this one for each plant discovered on the journey.

many branches for kindling, but enough of the trees remained so that he could harvest a vast quantity of seeds. However, just as Rock was finishing his work, he discovered a fresh set of tiger tracks. Now he had something else to worry about. Was it stalking him?

That night, a tiger attacked a nearby village, killing three women and a child. Soon after, a storm arose, with continual flashes of lightning and thunder, and a frightened herd of elephants stampeded through the village where Rock was staying, destroying almost everything in their path. Fortunately, Rock escaped with all the seeds he had gathered. From these seeds, a plantation of kalaw trees generated the much-needed *chaulmoogra* oil to treat leprosy.

Whole industries like rubber and tea have sprung from a single plant; dread diseases, such as malaria and leprosy, have finally come under control because of plants. What other undiscovered plants could help the human race? That is what plant hunters continue to search for—that rare, unknown plant with the potential to change human life.

CHAPTER 6

CONTEMPORARY PLANT GEEKS

TODAY, PLANT HUNTERS still travel to all the corners of the earth in search of new or hard-to-obtain plants. Even with a heavily populated planet, unexplored areas exist in places such as Papua New Guinea, Tibet, Cameroon, and South America. Travel conditions may be a bit easier for modern-day hunters, who sometimes enjoy the comforts of hotels, inns, and private homes, but like their predecessors, they scale dangerous cliffs, get trapped in flooded caves, find themselves stranded without food, walk the rims of volcanoes, and even have to outwit robbers. Some contemporary hunters work for universities, exploring remote pockets of the world for plants that will advance both science and medicine. Others work for environmental advocates, hoping to ensure the biodiversity of the planet. A few own plant nurseries and hunt for new plants for their customers.

Undiscovered plants still have the potential to make major contributions to our lives. The University of Montana professor Dr. Gary A. Strobel, called by *Forbes* magazine the Indiana Jones of fungus hunters, specializes in plant pathology and has located a fungus, *Gliocladium roseum*, on a tree in Chile's Patagonia area. He has determined that it can produce many of the same hydrocarbons found in diesel fuel and believes that with development it could become an energy source for automobiles. If so, it could help relieve world dependence on oil and become part of the solution to the energy crisis.

Other newly found plants simply increase the number of species that scientists know about and have cataloged, helping them understand the biodiversity of our planet. These new species sometimes emerge close to home. In 2001, the amateur photographer and naturalist John Pelton first noticed a small gentian in Arkansas, now named Pelton's rose gentian.

Most newly found plants, however, emerge from scientific expeditions to remote areas of the world—a species of ginger in Borneo; coffee in the highland forests of Cameroon; orchids in the "Green Corridor" of Vietnam; lilies and a begonia in Kathmandu, Nepal. In India alone, the botanic paradise that Joseph Hooker so loved, 167 new plants were found in 2008.

Scientists and volunteers traveling for organizations such as Earthwatch make yearly plant discoveries. Other "foot soldiers for biodiversity" support the efforts of the Svalbard Global Seed Vault, located on the Norwegian island of Spitsbergen. This carefully designed fortress, with airlocks and security cameras, has been built into a sandstone mountain. Here seeds gathered worldwide are being stored and can be kept viable for hundreds of years; some could survive for thousands. This huge collection, which has the capacity to store up to 225 billion seeds, could be used to help scientists find the genetic material they need to breed plants that will be resistant to future plant diseases. If Ireland's potato crop were hit with another crushing blight, the germplasm (genetic material) needed to create a blight-resistant potato could be located in this seed bank. If a regional or global crisis caused a mass destruction of plants, the vegetation of a particular area could be regrown from the seeds stored and protected here.

Today the possibility of bioterrorism has become a major threat to the world. A fungal spore so small that it could be hidden in a shoe could destroy the world's rubber plantations, shutting down production for years.

An exterior view of the Global Seed Vault at Svalbard. Cowpea seeds in Nigeria that will be shipped to the vault. Staff in Nigeria checking shipments headed to the vault. An interior view of the vault.

Seeds stored in Svalbard or one of the other 1,400 seed banks around the world provide insurance against such attacks. They would make it possible to regenerate the plants that sustain life on earth. For these important seed stockpiles, the hunters travel everywhere—Oman's mountains, the Sahara, the Caucasus, Turkmenistan, and North and South America—in search of seeds to protect.

These modern-day enthusiasts sometimes call themselves "plant geeks" and define their favorite plant as the one "in front of me at the moment."

A modern-day plant hunter, Richard H. Ree, preparing specimens in Tibet, China.

Daniel J. Hinkley, one of the best-known contemporary American plant hunters, has traveled in China, Japan, South Korea, Vietnam, Turkey, Nepal, Mexico, and Chile in search of species that will adapt well to American gardens. Hinkley became intrigued with plant hunting as a young man: "My earliest memories are of being fascinated with seeds and gathering plants in the woods and putting them on my windowsill. I remember germinating seeds in the kitchen, something I found irresistible—orange, grapefruit seeds, and avocadoes. I still have that same sensation when I see a seed come up. It is such a remarkable thing. It is a true miracle."

Hinkley became addicted to searching for plants as a teenager when he found a patch of original-growth eastern white cedar trees in his home state of Michigan. In his pursuit of plants, Hinkley shares the philosophy of most modern-day hunters: "My motto is to step lightly . . . Aldo Leopold in *Sand County Almanac* said that one cannot pluck a daisy without troubling a star. I remember that while I am out there. So I step as lightly as possible."

Today's "plant geeks" share the traits of those who came before them: a love of the natural world, the thrill of discovery and travel, and a dedication to botany and science. Their passion for plants, botanomania, still drives individuals to undertake exciting and exotic missions—all for the sake of a beautiful, unusual, useful, or rare plant. They are out there, still undiscovered. Ready to enthrall their first viewers. Waiting to be found.

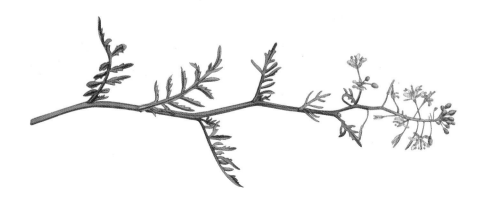

TIME LINE

1495 B.C.   Queen Hatshepsut of ancient Egypt sends out the first plant hunters.

A.D. 1600s   Tulips become the craze in the Netherlands—and vast fortunes are paid for rare tulip bulbs.

1700s–1900s   Thousands of plant hunters scour the planet to increase the vast botanic collections of Europe and America.

1700s   John Bartram of Philadelphia spends forty years hunting plants in North America.

Mid-1700s   Carl Linnaeus, the father of modern botany, begins cataloging plants.

1768–1771   Captain James Cook and Sir Joseph Banks travel around the world and explore Australia and New Zealand.

1800   Baron Alexander von Humboldt explores uncharted regions of Venezuela and Brazil.

1805   President Thomas Jefferson dispatches Meriwether Lewis and William Clark to travel across America.

1814	Humboldt publishes his journals as *Personal Narrative of a Journey to the Equinoctial Regions of the New Continent.*
1824	David Douglas begins expeditions in the Pacific Northwest.
1829	Dr. Nathaniel Bagshaw Ward accidentally discovers how to preserve plants by growing them in bottles.
1840	First patent issued for a camera.
1840s	William Colenso collects plants in Australia.
1840s	Robert Fortune travels in China as a plant hunter.
1847	Joseph Dalton Hooker begins his expedition to India.
1850s	Joseph Dalton Hooker helps Charles Darwin in his research.
1859	Charles Darwin publishes *On the Origin of Species.*
1860	Joseph Dalton Hooker requests that Richard Spruce harvest red cinchona trees.
1874	W. E. P. Giles travels in the vast deserts of central Australia.
1876	Henry Alexander Wickham transports rubber trees to England.
1870s	Benedict Roezl from Bohemia travels throughout Mexico and South America.
Early 1900s	Frank Meyer declares that he wants to "skim the earth in search of things good for man."
Early 1900s	Ernest H. Wilson travels in China for both James Veitch and Sons and the Arnold Arboretum.

Early 1900s   George Forrest travels in China's Hunan Province for the Edinburgh Botanic Garden in Scotland.

1914   Alice Eastwood travels to the Yukon for Harvard University.

1918   Frank Meyer dies on his last trip to China.

1919   Ernest H. Wilson becomes director of the Arnold Arboretum.

1920   Joseph F. Rock sets out to the Far East to find the plant that might cure leprosy.

1925   Ynés Mexía takes her first plant-hunting expedition.

2001   The amateur photographer and naturalist John Pelton notices a small gentian in Arkansas.

2006   Construction begins on the Svalbard Global Seed Vault.

2008   167 new plants located in India.

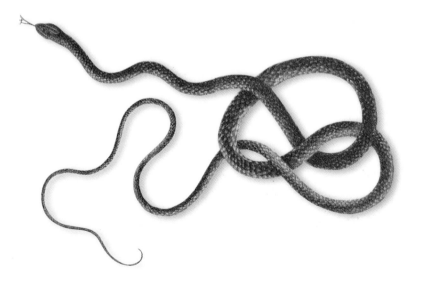

AUTHOR'S NOTE

THE EXPLORERS IN THIS BOOK roamed all over the world in search of plants. Their incredible bravery and tenacity amaze me.

But sometimes our greatest adventures take place within a few miles of home. Soon after coming to live in Boston, Massachusetts, in 1970, I began to explore its parks and nature preserves. I found, much to my delight, the beautiful shaded paths of the Arnold Arboretum. In this quiet spot in the middle of Jamaica Plain's busy streets, thousands of trees and shrubs have grown to maturity—marked with plaques that indicate their common and scientific names, their place of origin, the date of their discovery, and the name of the explorer who found them. Later I moved only a few miles away from the Arboretum, and visited it with my two Bernese mountain dogs, Lady and Merlin; they enjoyed it as much as I did, guided by endless, intriguing smells. But during these marvelous walks, I never thought much about the arboretum—how it came about or who created it.

Then, while writing *500 Great Books for Teens*, I came across a single paragraph in Susan Orlean's *The Orchid Thief* where she talked about plant hunters. "Plant hunters," I thought. "Who were the plant hunters?" The answer to that question led to five years of research. During that time, I made my first visit to the Arnold Arboretum library; many of the volumes written or commissioned by these explorers can be found there—some of them hundreds of years old and bound in beautiful leather.

My journey on this book ended at the arboretum library as well. There I sat with my editor, Melanie Kroupa, and worked with the librarian Lisa Pearson to secure reproductions of the images I wanted to use in *The Plant Hunters*. Lisa located so many pictures unknown to me because of her encyclopedic knowledge of the arboretum collection, as well as those of other botanic libraries, such as Harvard's Gray Herbarium. She even photographed some of the undigitized sources. By this point, snow clogged the arboretum pathways, but inside the warm and spacious research room Melanie and I looked through a host of treasures. My favorite, discovered at this stage, was the photograph of Ernest H. Wilson with "reformed headhunters" on page 29. How, I wondered, did Wilson know they were "reformed"?

This book describes daredevil adventures, breathtaking escapes, near-death experiences; I learned about all of them at a library near my house. That is what libraries do—they allow you to travel geographically and across time. They open up the whole world. They are the next best thing to a trip down the Amazon.

Color photograph of Dawson Pond by Corliss Engle at the Arnold Arboretum, Jamaica Plain, Massachusetts.

NOTES

"Botanomania": A Passion for Plants

5   *"The mere suspicion"*: Whittle, p. 58.

5   *"extremes of heat"*: Ibid., p. 70.

Chapter 1   The Indiana Jones of the Nineteenth Century

6   *"I walked along"*: Humboldt, pp. 184–85.

7   *"What magnificent vegetation"*: Bruhns, p. 26.

7   *The rain forests of Venezuela*: Humboldt, pp. 79, 83–84.

10   *15 percent of the world's*: Helferich, p. 110.

10   *cabin . . . "the dog"*: Helferich, p. 112.

10   *a floating zoo*: Humboldt, p. 243; Sachs, p. 164; Smith, p. 241.

10–12   *During the day . . . established a camp*: Humboldt, pp. 160–78, 199.

12   *the baron's hands to swell*: Helferich, p. 138.

12   *"However much you try"*: Humboldt, p. 208.

12   *To counteract the insects*: Helferich, p. 62.

12   *hornitos*: Humboldt, pp. 209–10.

13   *Brazil nut tree*: Ibid., p. 258.

14   *piranha*: Helferich, pp. 119–20.

15   *"Even if we had gained the shore"*: Bruhns, p. 279.

16   *"kills silently"*: Humboldt, p. 253.

16   *accidentally spilled*: Ibid., p. 257.

16   *feared that Bonpland had died*: Bruhns, pp. 279–88.

CHAPTER 2 Why Did They Do It?

17   *shared similar characteristics*: Whittle, p. 100.

18   *"I don't mind"*: Bonta, pp. 93–102.

19   *"a task where I"*: Ibid., p. 114.

19   *"the little botanist"*: Healey, p. 54.

19   *His need to organize*: Gribbin and Gribbin, p. 34.

19   *Sweden's rugged Lapland region*: Ibid., p. 36.

20   *Linnaeus's system . . . could be mastered quickly*: Ibid., p. 44.

20   *Linnaeus renamed it* Rosa: Whittle, pp. 45–50.

20   *"apostles"*: Gribbin and Gribbin, p. 57.

22   *"permanent exhibits under my name"*: Bonta, p. 106.

22   *Mexianthus mexicanus*: Ibid., pp. 105–6.

23   *searching for unusual specimens*: Whittle, pp. 51–55.

23   *but also a plant hunter*: Ibid., pp. 87–90.

23   *Cape Disappointment*: Musgrave, Gardner, and Musgrave, p. 62.

24   *a splitting headache*: Ibid., p. 67.

26   *prized harvest*: Whittle, pp. 94–97.

26   *"The greatest service"*: Ward, p. 295.

26   *"skim the earth"*: Cunningham, p. 5.

26   *He found wheat*: Fairchild, p. 57.

26   *"by the wayside"*: Musgrave, Gardner, and Musgrave, p. 169.

28   *"Then it was"*: Ibid., p. 171.

29   *"lily limp"*: Whittle, pp. 4–5.

CHAPTER 3 Bringing the Plants Home Alive

32   *crabapple trees in Asia*: Ward, pp. 18–19.

32   *specimen as a scientific record*: Short, p. 222.

34   *Hollywood extravaganza*: Hooker, pp. 169–71.

34 *poked their heads into Hooker's tent*: Orlean, pp. 59–60.

36 *working sixteen to eighteen hours*: Hooker, p. 180.

36 *"lassitude, headache, and giddiness"*: Ibid., p. 211.

37 *he was always sick*: Allan, p. 174.

37 *"a dense drizzling fog"*: Hooker, pp. 241–42.

39 *the plant's genetic resources*: Whittle, pp. 109–11.

39 *eaten by insects*: Desmond, p. 170; Allan, p. 183.

39 *Transporting living plant stock*: Whittle, pp. 109–11.

39 *weather and temperature changes*: Ibid., p. 112.

41 *the boat more stable*: Ibid., pp. 113–14.

41 *transporting of plants for several thousand years*: Ibid., p. 111.

42 *rhododendrons from India*: Ibid., pp. 122–29.

CHAPTER 4 Bringing Themselves Home Alive

44 *never reached the fort*: Short, pp. 175–78.

46 *"do not stop at the toes"*: Ibid., pp. 287–88.

46 *referred to it as "infernal"*: Ibid., pp. 148–49.

47 *to find another victim*: Whittle, pp. 145–47.

48 *some by poison arrows*: Short, p. 110.

48 *collect a single specimen*: Musgrave, Gardner, and Musgrave, p. 187.

49 *"I lost everything I possessed"*: Whittle, pp. 245–48; Short, pp. 110–14.

CHAPTER 5 Plant Superstars

52 *a suit of clothes*: Healey, p. 12.

55 *more than Wickham*: Allan, pp. 205–6, 230; Whittle, pp. 11–12.

55 *brave and determined botanist*: Whittle, p. 189.

56 *harvesting tea*: Gribbin and Gribbin, p. 207.

57 *China in the tea industry*: Whittle, p. 191; Gribbin, p. 4.

57 *"The rains set in"*: Musgrave and Musgrave, p. 153.

59 *cinchona trees growing there*: Ibid., p. 153.

59 *moistened strips of calico*: Healey, p. 121.

59 *deadly disease of malaria*: Dodge, pp. 206–14.

60 *"was going to beat"*: Allan, p. 200.

60 *"his two best"*: Appleman, p. 68.

62 chaulmoogra . . . *leprosy*: Whittle, pp. 228–31; Dodge, pp. 223–29.

Chapter 6 Contemporary Plant Geeks

66 *solution to the energy crisis*: Chadwick.

66 *Pelton's rose gentian*: Arkansas Natural Heritage Commission.

66 *167 new plants were found*: "167 New Plant Species Discovered in India."

66 *seeds stored and protected*: Rosner.

67 *"in front of me"*: Ward, p. 76.

69 *American gardens*: Ibid., pp. 154–63.

69 *"My earliest memories"*: Hinkley, interview with the author.

69 *"My motto is"*: Ibid.

BIBLIOGRAPHY

Allan, Mea. *The Hookers of Kew.* London: Michael Joseph, 1967.

Appleman, Philip, ed. *Darwin.* Norton Critical Editions. New York: W. W. Norton, 2000.

Arkansas Natural Heritage Commission. www.naturalheritage.com/news-events.

Bonta, Marcia Myers. *Women in the Field.* College Station: Texas A&M University Press, 1991.

Bruhns, Karl. *Life of Alexander von Humboldt.* London: Longmans, Green, 1873.

Chadwick, Alex. "Day to Day." National Public Radio. November 4, 2008.

Cunningham, Isabel Shipley. *Frank N. Meyer: Plant Hunter in Asia.* Ames: Iowa State University Press, 1984.

Desmond, Raymond. *Sir Joseph Dalton Hooker.* Woodbridge, England: Antique Collector's Club, 1999.

Dodge, Bertha. *It Started in Eden.* New York: McGraw-Hill, 1979.

Fairchild, Douglas. "A Hunter of Plants." *National Geographic* 36 (1919).

Gribbin, John, and Mary Gribbin. *Flower Hunters.* London: Oxford University Press, 2009.

Healey, B. J. *The Plant Hunters.* New York: Charles Scribner's, 1975.

Helferich, Gerard. *Humboldt's Cosmos.* New York: Gotham Books, 2004.

Hinkley, Daniel J. *The Explorer's Garden: Rare and Unusual Perennials.* Portland, Oregon: Timber Press, 1999.

———. Interview with the author. June 19, 2008.

Hooker, Sir Joseph. *Himalayan Journals.* Volumes I and II. London: John Murray, 1855.

Humboldt, Alexander von. *Personal Narrative of a Journey to the Equinoctial Regions of the New Continent.* 1814; reprint New York: Penguin Books, 1995.

Lindsay, Ann, and Syd House. *The Tree Collector: The Life and Explorations of David Douglas.* London: Aurum Press, 1999.

Moore, Patricia Ann. *Cultivating Science in the Field: Alice Eastwood, Ynés Mexía and California Botany, 1890–1940.* Ann Arbor: University of Michigan, 1997.

Musgrave, Toby, Chris Gardner, and Will Musgrave. *The Plant Hunters: Two Hundred Years of Adventure and Discovery Around the World.* London: Ward Lock Ltd., 1999.

Musgrave, Toby, and Will Musgrave. *An Empire of Plants: People and Plants That Changed the World.* London: Cassell, 2001.

"167 New Plant Species Discovered in India." *The Hindu*, June 8, 2009.

Orlean, Susan. *The Orchid Thief*. New York: Ballantine Books, 2000.

Rosner, Hilary. "Seeds to Save a Species." *Popular Science*, April 1, 2008.

Sachs, Aaron. *The Humboldt Current*. New York: Viking Press, 2006.

Scottish Rock Garden Club. *The Rock Garden* 114 (January 2005).

Short, Philip. *In Pursuit of Plants*. Portland, Oregon: Timber Press, 2003.

Smith, Anthony. *Explorers of the Amazon*. Chicago: University of Chicago Press, 1990.

Ward, Bobby J. *The Plant Hunter's Garden*. Portland, Oregon: Timber Press, 2004.

Whittle, Tyler. *The Plant Hunters*. Philadelphia: Chilton Book Company, 1970.

ILLUSTRATION CREDITS

INDEX

Note: numbers in italics indicate illustrations.

Aceraceae, *64*
Aciphylla colensoi, 46
altitude sickness, 36–37, 60
Amazon, 10, 12, 45, 74
Amazonas (ship), 53
Andes Mountains, 57
Arnold Arboretum (Boston), 26, 29, *30, 33*, 71
Asia, 32, 52
    see also China; India; Tibet
Australia, 5, 43–44, 46, 70, 71

bamboo, 13
banana trees, 7
bandits, 46–47
Bangkok (Thailand), 63
Banks, Joseph, 5, 70
Bartram, John, 22–23, 70
bear grass, 4
bears, 3, 45
begonias, 32, 66

Benares (India), 62
biodiversity, 65, 66
bioterrorism, 66
birdfoot violets, 22
Bligh, Captain William, 5
Bohemia, 46, 71
Bonpland, Pierre, 6, 10, 12–13, 15, 16
Borneo, 66
botany, 4, 18, 19, 41, 69, 70
Bounty (ship), 5
Brazil, 6, 53–54, 70
Brazil nuts, *13*, 13–14
breadfruit, 5
buckthorn, false, 4
Buddhist monks, 47–48
bulbs, 26, 52

California Academy of Sciences, 18
cameras, 37, 71
Cameroon, 65, 66
Capel, Lord of Tewkesbury, 21

capybaras, 12

Caucasus, 67

cedar trees, 4, 69

Central America, 19

    map of, *11*

Ceylon, 55, 56, 59

chaulmoogra oil, 62, 64

cherry trees, 26, *30*, 32

chestnuts, Malabar, 13

Chile, 65, 69

China, 3, 17, 47, 72

    Fortune in, *54*, 55, *56*, 71

    Meyer in, *18*, 26, 50, 51, *51*

    tea plants in, 52, 55–57

    Wilson in, 26–29, *28*, 71

Chow-hai Ting, *18*

cinchona trees, 52, 57, *58*, 59, 71

Clark, William, 4, 70

classification system, 19–20

cockroaches, 45

coconut palms, 7

coffee, 66

Colenso, William, 46, 71

Collinson, Peter, 22–23

Columbia River, 23

Cook, Captain James, 4–5, 70

cougars, 45

cowpea seeds, *67*

cow trees, 13

crabapple trees, 32

crocodiles, 6, 7, 12, 15, 17

crops, commercial, 5, 26, 50, 55

Cumaná (Venezuela), 16

curare, 15–16

daffodils, 32

Darwin, Charles, 60, 71

    On the Origin of Species, 60, *61*, 71

disease-resistant plants, 66

dog rose, 20

Douglas, David, 23–26, *24*, 71

Douglas fir, 26

East India Company, 55

Eastwood, Alice, 18, 72

Ecuador, 3, 57, 59

Edinburgh Botanic Garden, 47, 72

Edwards, Amelia, 4

Egypt, ancient, 3, 39, 70

elephants, 64

energy sources, 65–66

England, 21, 26, 42, 54–55, 71

    Horticultural Society of, 23

    Royal Botanical Gardens of,

      see Kew Gardens

    Victorian, 52

environmental advocacy, 65–66

equipment

    plant-harvesting, 32

    scientific, 6–7

evolution, Darwin's theory of, 60

false buckthorn, 4

ferns, 41

fever bark trees, *see* cinchona trees

fir, Douglas, 26

Fitch, Walter Hood, *38, 42, 59*

flamingos, 12

forestry industry, 26

Formosa, *29*

Forrest, George, *47*, 47–49, 72

Fort McKellar (Australia), 43–44

Fortune, Robert, 55–56, 72
   Three Years' Wanderings in the Northern Provinces of China, *54*, 56

frankincense trees, 3

fungus, 22, 65–66

genetic material, 39, 66

gentians, 48, 66, 72

geraniums, 32

germplasm, 39, 66

Giles, W. E. P., 43–44, 71

ginger, 66

Gliocladium roseum, 65–66

grasses, 41

Harvard University, 18, 72
   see also Arnold Arboretum

Hatshepsut, Queen of Egypt, 3, *4*, 70

headache trees, 24

herons, 6, 12

Hevea brasiliensis, 53

Himalayas, *36*, 36–37, *38*, *40*, 56, 60

Hinkley, Daniel J., 69

Hooker, Joseph Dalton, 5, *35*, 52–53, 55, 57
   Darwin and, 60, 71
   Himalayan Journals, 36, *38*, 44
   India expedition of, 33–39, 42, 66, 71
   Rhododendrons of Sikkim-Himalaya, The, *40*, 42

Howard, John Eliot, *59*

Humboldt, Baron Alexander von, 5–17, *7*, 70, 71
   map drawn by, *10–11*
   Personal Narrative of a Journey to the Equinoctial Regions of the New Continent, 7, 71

hyacinths, 32

India, *36*, 66, 72
   cinchona plantations in, 59
   Hooker's expedition to, 33–39, 42, *44*, 66, 71
   leprosy in, 62
   tea plantations in, 55, 57

Indonesia, 63

insects, 7, 12, 45, 57

Irish potato famine, 66

Jacob's ladder, 4

jaguars, 7, 10, 12, 17

Jalisco (Mexico), 22

Japan, 69

Jefferson, Thomas, 4, 26, 70

Kalapooia tribe, 23–25

kalaw trees, 62–64

Kathmandu (Nepal), 66

Kew Gardens (London), 21, 33, 39, 42, 45, 53, 54, 57

Khasia Hills (India), *36*

Lapland, 19

Latin names, 20

Leopold, Aldo, 69
leprosy, 62–64, 72
Lewis, Meriwether, 4, 70
Lhasa (Tibet), 47
lianas, 10
lilies, 26, 48, 66
Limón (Ecuador), 57
Linden, Jean Jules, 2
Linnaeus, Carl, 19–20, 57, 70
    Flora Lapponica, 21, 22
living plant stock, transporting,
    39–42, 59
Lusitania (ship), 50

Malabar chestnuts, 13
malaria, 5, 52, 57, 59, 64
medicinal plants, 5, 52, 57–59,
    62–65
Mekong River, 48
Mexía, Ynés, 5, 19, 22, 72
Mexianthus mexicanus, 22
Mexico, 22, 46, 69, 71
    map of, *11*
Meyer, Frank Nicholas, 5, 49–52,
    71, 72
    in China, *18*, 26, 50, 51, *51*
    in Turkistan, *49*
milk trees, 13
Mimosa mexiae, 22
Min Valley (China), 36
Mongolia, 17
monkey flower, 4
monkeys, 10, 12, 14, 56, 63
Montana, University of, 65

mosquitoes, 12, 57
Mount Chimboazo, *8–9*
Multnomah River, 23

Nepal, 66, 69
nerve poison, 15–16
Netherlands, 52, 70
New Zealand, 5, 70
North America, 22–23, 26, 67, 70
    immigrant plants in, 32
    see also United States
Norway, 66

Oman, 67
orchids, 2, 10, 32, 39, 46, 52, 66
Orinoco River, 3, 10, 15

panthers, 12
Papua New Guinea, 65
parrots, 14
pelicans, 12
Pelton, John, 66, 72
pheasants, 12
Philippines, 3
pines, sugar, 23, 25–26
Pinus lambertiana, 23, *25*, 25–26
piranhas, 14–15, 17
pirates, 55
plant classification, 19–20
porcupines, 63
potatoes, 66
primulas, 48
Punt, 3, *4*

quinine, 5, 59

rabbitbush, 4
rain forest, Venezuelan, 7, 10–16
rain trees, 13
Ray, John, 19
red cedar, 4
Ree, Richard H., *68*
regal lily, 26
Rhododendron
    R. barbatum, 42
    R. dahlousie, 40
rhododendrons, *40*, 42, *42*
Rock, Joseph F., 5, 62–64, *62, 63*, 72
    specimen book of, *64*
Roezl, Benedict, 46–47, 71
Roman Catholic Church, 59
Rosa canina, 20
rubber trees, 5, *53*, 53–55, 64, 66

Sahara, 67
Sandler, Frederick, and Son, 52
Sargent, Charles Sprague, *30*
sauba ants, 45
saxifrages, 48
scientific instruments, 6–7
scientific revolution, 19
Scone Palace (Scotland), 23
scorpions, 45
Scotland, 23, 47, 72
seed banks, 66–67, *67*
seeds, 23–24, 39, 69
    for medicinal plants, 57, 59,
        63–64

    for rubber trees, 53–54
    for tea plants, 55
Sierra Leone, 3
sloths, 12
South Africa, 32
South America, 19, 32, 46, 53, 65,
    67, 71
    Humboldt's expedition to, 5–17,
        8–9, 14, 70
    Kew Gardens plant hunters in,
        53, 57
South Korea, 69
soybeans, 52
specimens, plant, 5, 19, 23, 43, 54
    gathering, 6, 10, 39, 59
    loss of, 15, 45
    preserving, 13, 32, *34, 37, 64, 68*
    transporting, 39–42, 59–60
Spitsbergen, 66
spoonbills, 12
Spruce, Richard, *45*, 45–46, 57,
    59, 71
squirrels, 14
Sri Lanka, *see* Ceylon
Strobel, Gary A., 65
sugar pines, 23, 25–26
Svalbard Global Seed Vault, 66–67,
    67, 72
Sweden, 19

Tahiti, 5
tea plants, 52, 55–57, 64
termites, 45
Tibet, 47–49, *62, 63, 65, 68*

tigers, 6, 7, 15, 64
Tikuna tribe, 15
Titanic (ship), 50
Tournefort, Joseph, 19–20
trees, 10
    banana, 7
    cedar, 4, 69
    cherry, 26, *30*, 32
    chestnut, 13
    cinchona, 52, 57, *58*, 59, 71
    coconut palm, 7
    cow, 13
    crabapple, 32
    fir, 26
    frankincense, 3
    headache, 24
    kalaw, 62–64
    milk, 13
    pine, 23, 25–26
    rain, 13
    rubber, 5, *53*, 53–55, 64, 66
tulips, 32, 52, 70
Turkey, 69
Turkistan, 17, 49
Turkmenistan, 67

Umbellularia californica, 24
United States, 22–26, 49, 66, 69, 72

Department of Agriculture, 26, 50, 52, 63
    immigrant plants in, 32, 50
Uppsala, University of, 19

vampire bats, 3, 45–46
Varanasi (India), 62
vasculum, 32, *33*
Veitch, James, and Sons nursery, 26, 71
Venezuela, 6, 7, 10–16, 70
Vietnam, 66, 69
vines, climbing, 10
violets, birdfoot, 22

Ward, Nathaniel Bagshaw, 41, 71
Wardian cases, *41*, 41–42, 55
Weitsch, Friedrich Georg, 7
wheat, 26
white cedar, 79
Wickham, Henry Alexander, 52–55, 71
Wilson, Ellen Garderton, 27
Wilson, Ernest H., 26–31, *27–30*, 71
    vasculum and notebook of, *33*

yaks, 34–35
Yangtze River, 3, 51
Yukon, 18, 72

zamang (rain tree), 13